# Summary of: HAPPY GUT

*THE CLEANSING PROGRAM TO HELP YOU LOSE WEIGHT GAIN ENERGY, AND ELIMINATE PAIN*

## By: Dr. Vincent Pedre

**Summarized by:**
**Knowledge House**

© 2018

## © Copyright 2018 by Knowledge House

**All rights reserved.**

This document is geared toward providing exact and reliable information in regard to the topic and issue covered. The publication is sold with the idea that the publisher is not required to render accounting, officially permitted, or otherwise, qualified services. If advice is necessary, legal or professional, a practiced individual in the profession should be ordered.

- From a Declaration of Principles which was accepted and approved equally by a Committee of the American Bar Association and a Committee of Publishers and Associations.

In no way is it legal to reproduce, duplicate, or transmit any part of this document in either electronic means or in printed format. Recording of this publication is strictly prohibited and any storage of this document is not allowed unless with written permission from the publisher. All rights reserved.

The information provided herein is stated to be truthful and consistent, in that any liability, in terms of inattention or otherwise, by any usage or abuse of any policies, processes, or directions contained within is the solitary and utter responsibility of the recipient reader. Under no circumstances will any legal responsibility or blame be held against the publisher for any reparation, damages, or monetary loss due to the information herein, either directly or indirectly.

Respective authors own all copyrights not held by the publisher.

The information herein is offered for informational purposes solely, and is universal as so. The presentation of the information is without contract or any type of guarantee assurance.

The trademarks that are used are without any consent, and the publication of the trademark is without permission or backing by the trademark owner. All trademarks and brands within this book are for clarifying purposes only and are the owned by the owners themselves, not affiliated with this document.

# TABLE OF CONTENTS

**INTRODUCTION** .................................................................. 5

**PART I: IT'S ALL ABOUT THE GUT** ........................... 11

   1. IT'S ALL IN YOUR GUT ................................................. 12
   2. THE HAPPY GUT DIET: PHASE I EXPLAINED ........... 23

**PART II: THE GUT C.A.R.E. PROGRAM: TWENTY-EIGHT DAYS TO A NEW YOU** ...................................... 37

   1. ELIMINATE SYMPTOMS AND MAINTAIN YOUR HEALTH WITH THE GUT C.A.R.E. PROGRAM ................. 38
   2. TIPS FOR SUCCESS: CREATING A HAPPY GUT .......... 57

**PART III: REINTRODUCTION PHASE AND FURTHER TESTING** ........................................................ 61

   1. REINTRODUCTION AND YOUR GUT C.A.R.E. PLAN FOR LIFE ........................................................................ 62
   2. FURTHER TESTING FOR GUT-RELATED AILMENTS ..................................................................... 65

**PART IV: A HAPPY GUT, HAPPY LIFE** ..................... 77

   1. THE EMOTIONAL GUT: THE MIND-GUT CONNECTION ................................................................. 78
   2. THE PHYSICAL GUT: THE BODY-GUT CONNECTION ................................................................. 86

**CONCLUSION** ................................................................. 91

# INTRODUCTION

The health of your gut is way more important than you think. The gastrointestinal system isn't only used for absorbing food and getting rid of waste, but it also controls your immune system. It even has its nervous system which means that it stays in constant contact with your brain thus affecting your mood and overall function.

Your gut also contains trillions of microbiomes, and they have a significant impact on your health. Finally, it also functions as a detoxifier, getting rid of toxins from food and the environment. So everything from your weight, mood or energy is regulated through your gut.

This book will work as a practical guide to help you obtain optimal gut health and thus improve every single aspect of your life.

Let me begin you by telling a story, a young mid-20's patient of mine came to me with symptoms of bloating, gas and irregular bowel movements. She said to me that she had a pretty bad diet during her college years, and her symptoms started then but have got worse over the years. She had already seen quite a few doctors who did her bloodwork and colonoscopy and found nothing unusual and sent her home and told her that her symptoms are probably due to high-stress levels.

Do you know a similar story? Maybe you can even relate to that young woman because you suffer from the symptoms. The problem is even more severe because very few doctors are educated in the nutritional space and have no clue about proper gut health. When I was going to medical school, nutritional knowledge was simply taught over a few lectures as a side note.

My gut troubles began when I was a kid and had an upset stomach. Whenever I had a bid exam or had to speak in front of a large crowd, I would feel sick in my stomach. I had poor digestion, and my immune system was wreckage. It was when I moved away from home and had to prepare the food that I realized how much it was impacting my overall well being. I started making better choices, but I was still following a regular western diet full of wheat. My staple was pizza and pop just like a typical American student, what a deadly combo!

I started experimenting a bit with organic foods and noticed that my energy level increased sharply when I began consuming lean meats and fresh vegetables. But that wasn't enough I wanted to heal my gut, and that's what this book is going to do for you.

First of all, we need to establish why your gut isn't performing very well?

So here's a breakdown of the book:

Part I talks about how your gut became unhappy in the first place?

Chapter 1 talks the imbalance in your gut and how you can fix it in 28 days.

Chapter 2 talks about better food choices.

Part II talks about rebooting your gut with the C.A.R.E. system.

Chapter 3 talks about a comprehensive diet plan.

Chapter 4 talks about how to stay on the program and succeed.

Part III talks about food reintroduction phase.

Chapter 5 talks about how to eat after the diet program.
Chapter 6 talks about many hidden causes of common diseases.

Part IV talks about the mental and emotional side effects of having an unhappy gut.

Chapter 7 talks about why is our gut called our second brain and also discusses alternative healing methods.

Chapter 8 talks about the importance of physical exercise and meditation.

So let's begin our journey together towards a better and happier gut!

# PART I

# IT'S ALL ABOUT THE GUT

# 1. IT'S ALL IN YOUR GUT

Have you ever had that experience where you haven't gone to the bathroom to relieve yourself for days? You wake up with a foggy head, and you're tired although you've been sleeping for hours? You feel bloated, have sore joints and can't concentrate at all. You will be surprised to know that the root of your problem is an out of balance gut.

So what is a gut? Your gut is just like a garden and requires similar attention. It is in constant interaction with food, toxins, additives, microbes, etc. Its job is to keep all the bad stuff out of your body and let the right things get absorbed. The bacteria in the gut help us digest food, create vitamins. It also sends a signal to your brain to tell you that you are full and finally it enables you to release toxins and waste through your rectum via stool.

A gut is healthy when all the food is digested

properly, and it can absorb nutrients properly. And that the immune system of your gut is functioning well.

What is digestion?

Digestion starts when you put something in your mouth and start chewing, the saliva breaks down carbohydrates and then the food goes into the stomach where enzymes are released which begin breaking down protein. It also defends against bacteria.

Carbohydrates are broken down into glucose while protein is converted into amino acids. Then food travels to the small intestine where a high pH environment is used for fat absorption. The bacteria in our small intestine live off the food that we eat and help us break it down. Finally, the food travels down to the colon where the waste and toxins are used to create a final product i.e. stool.

Let's take a look at a few critical players during this process:

Liver: It produces bile which helps to absorb fat better. It also contributes significantly to detoxifying your body.

Gallbladder: It also produces bile and releases it into the small intestine during a meal.

Pancreas: It releases an alkaline juice to neutralize our stomach and also releases insulin which regulates blood sugar levels.

A healthy gut is supposed to perform the following five functions:

1. Digest food properly
2. Absorb all the nutrients
3. Maintain an immune barrier
4. Create and promote healthy bacteria
5. Detoxify your body of toxins

From the moment we are born through our mothers' bodies, we begin the process of colonizing our body with bacteria. These colonies change throughout our lives through our lifestyles, the food we consume, etc. These trillions of microbes dictate how we feel and how our immune systems work.

Unfortunately, the average American diet which is full of toxins such as sugar and junk food creates harmful bacteria in your gut. Every single disease starts in your gut. Western medicine is to be blamed for our gut issues as well, as doctors traditionally try to treat symptoms instead of looking at the cause of the ailment. On the other hand, functional medicine believes in the ability of the body to heal itself, and it treats the human body as a system. We'll discuss that in detail in later chapters.

Now back to your gut.

If you want to the real cause of what is happening inside you, you should be paying closer attention to what you're putting inside your body on a day to day basis. For example, if you eat a large soda with pizza and some wings, you will activate inflammation in your body whereas if you eat kale, you'll activate anticancer genes. The old saying that you're what you eat is true.

But here's the thing, processed food is cheap and incredibly addictive. The food industry doesn't care about your leaky gut, and all they want to do is make bigger profits. They have scientists to engineer food in a way that tastes so damn irresistible. They also use deceiving labels like low fat to damage us further. I'd highly recommend that you watch the documentary "Super Size Me," to see the amount of damage that could be done by eating processed foods every day.

One of the biggest poison of choice for many people is sugar. Now some people might say that they don't eat a lot of sugar. Well, do you consume pasta, bread, and cereal? They get converted into sugar inside your stomach. You might also be drinking commercial fruit juices thinking they are right for you, but they are also ridden with sugar.

The only way to feel healthy is by not

consuming these foods, and I'll help you do that. I'll also help you overcome the psychological barriers of food addiction.

Stress could also be a reason that your gut is unhappy. It has been shown in the studies that stress changes the balance of healthy bacteria in your gut. It is very important to find some time in your daily routine to wind down and relieve your stress. I recommend yoga and meditation to my patients, and we'll further talk about it in later chapters.

Then we have the serious issue of antibiotics. Many people rush to pop those antibiotics on the first sign of cold, little do they know that they are destroying their gut flora. And even once you stop taking antibiotics, if you don't repopulate your gut flora with right foods you suffer from the consequences of having an imbalanced gut flora.

So with the combination of making wrong food choices, consumption of antibiotics and our increasingly toxic environment no wonder there are so many sick people. After a few days to a few months of exposure to all these toxins, you develop a leaky gut which means that your body is exposed to partially digested protein molecules from food. The immune system becomes hyper active to fight these which results in all sorts of allergies and immune diseases.

Leaky gut is the bridge between gut health and major illnesses. Usually in a healthy gut, food is absorbed through the lining and cell wall of your gut, but in the case of a leaky gut, our immune is exposed to a plethora of substances that otherwise would not have come into contact with it.

So how is a leaky gut developed?

There are many reasons, ranging from:

- Bad diet
- Stress
- Infections
- Inflammation

- Low stomach acid
- Toxins
- Antibiotics

Our immune system is always guarding our gut to prevent any ailments. As it faces these alien particles, it attacks them and causes a burden on the immune system which later becomes an autoimmune disease. As you keep on eating incompletely digested foods on a daily basis, you begin to develop immune reactions to those foods.

Here are some of the symptoms of an overactive immune system:

- Bloating
- Constipation
- Fatigue
- Weight gain

If you are always eating food that you are sensitive to and have a leaky gut, then you will have water retention which will eventually lead to weight gain if left untreated.

Weight loss is effortless and happens automatically once you remove allergic foods in your diet.

Gut bacteria can even make you fat as it regulates our blood sugar levels and also tells us when we should feel satiated from our food. In one study gut bacteria from an obese person was transferred into mice who despite any change in its eating behavior gained an enormous amount of weight. A diversified gut bacteria is vital for maintaining a healthy mind and body. Due to the recent surge in the consumption of junk food in recent years, out gut bacteria is quickly becoming less diversified.

A plant-based diet creates a very well diversified gut bacterial environment.

A gut induced overactive immune system could lead to fat gain, skin issues, headaches and even depression.

In recent studies, gut issues have even been

associated with certain types of cancer. Stomach cancer is the third most common cause of cancer deaths.

## The Gut C.A.R.E. Program

Through my years of practice, I've developed a system to create a reboot program for optimal gut health.

**C**leanse
**A**ctivate
**R**estore
**E**nhance

It is a system designed to give you back your gut health no matter how damaged it is currently. And by fixing our gut, we fix plenty of issues in our body.

I believe in the ability of our body to heal itself when we create optimal balance in our gut we begin the process of healing ourselves.

Here is the system explained in a little more detail:

Cleanse: Get rid of toxins in your food.

Activate: Add essential nutrients in your food.

Restore: Reintroduce healthy bacteria in your gut.

Enhance: Repair the intestinal lining.

With this program, your gut will heal. You will get rid of excess weight, bloating and pain. Not only that but your skin will look better, and you will also feel and look younger.

Also, I will suggest that you keep track of how you are feeling currently and also make a note of your condition after you finish the program. It is essential to keep track of our symptoms and to see where we can make improvements.

Please consider leaving a review if you're enjoying this title.
Thanks.

# 2. THE HAPPY GUT DIET: PHASE I EXPLAINED

Now that you understand how our gut flora affects us and how the gut C.A.R.E. program can help you improve your gut, in this chapter we are going to take a look at specific food groups and how they are affecting you.

**Sugar**

Let's begin with discussing sugar. Let's make one thing clear, sugar is a killer, and it's one of the biggest culprits of the modern day epidemic of diseases.

Issues such as:

- Diabetes
- Depression
- Migraines
- Body aches
- Heart problems etc

When you consume too much sugar, it increases your blood pressure and heart rate and gives you a heightened sense of energy, but that soon comes crashing down once your insulin levels control your blood sugar. It even increases cortisol (stress hormone) which has been associated with further weight gain. And worse of all, you crave sugar just like a drug. In rat studies, it has been shown to be more addictive than cocaine.

The first thing that we need to discuss with sugar addiction is that why the person is consuming so much sugar? Is it because of a stressful job or are you treating some other underlying issues with sugar?

But there's hope, and gut C.A.R.E. program can help you get rid of your sugar addiction.

So what about artificial sugars? Well, they are equally as bad as sugar. I'd ask you to avoid any diet sodas and wherever you might find artificial sweeteners.

# Gluten

When I discuss with my patients that they will have to give up gluten (wheat), they are always very resisting. Things like bread and pasta have been so ingrained our culture that they are almost impossible to get rid of entirely.

So what exactly is gluten? It's a protein that gives bread their texture. It is said that as much as thirty percent of the American population might be allergic to gluten.

It can cause:

- Weight gain
- Mental fog
- Fatigue
- Pain
- Constipation etc

You can get tested for gluten sensitivity in the labs, but the best way to check for it is to get rid of it completely from your diet and see how you feel. You will have to give yourself at least two weeks before making any conclusions. Most of my patients are amazed by how quickly they feel less bloated.

Gluten isn't only in wheat but also in oats, barley, rye to name a few. It's used in several sauces and is even included in burgers. And you have to be careful about consuming some personal care products as it is added to them as well.

And don't think that because you don't have celiac disease or some other autoimmune diseases that you are free from gluten allergies. Many such people are suffering from an attack on their nervous system and joints.

Gluten might also be slowing down your metabolism which will lead to difficulty losing weight.

Ok, so you're ready to give up gluten to give your gut a chance to heal itself but hear me out before you go to the gluten-free aisle of your favorite supermarket. It's because most of the gluten-free products are laden with sugar and refined carbs.

I want you to start eating whole foods such as lean parts of meat, non-processed carbs, vegetables, and nuts.

## Dairy

Pasteurized milk doesn't have the necessary enzymes to digest milk properly for human consumption. Also, milk contains a sugar known as lactose which is hard to absorb for a lot of people and can cause bloating, gas and diarrhea.

Best alternatives to milk are:

- Rice milk
- Nut milk
- Coconut milk
- Hemp milk

Another reason to avoid dairy might be to have great glowing skin without any acne. A lot of my patients started clearing up after they stopped consuming dairy. Dairy has harmful hormones like bovine growth hormone which has been shown to increase the risk of colon, breast and prostate cancer.

**Eggs**

You'll be surprised to know that many people develop an allergic reaction to eggs over their lifetime. Eggs also create inflammation in our bodies. But not all inflammation is bad, and the main key is to have the right balance of omega-3s (anti-inflammatory) and omega-6s (pro-inflammatory). Egg yolk is full of omega 6s, so that's why they are not part of the anti-inflammatory diet. Hens that are raised on soy and corn produce eggs that are full of inflammation.

Organic eggs which are rich in omega 3s can be consumed after you are done with the elimination phase of the happy gut diet.

## Soy

There has been a recent surge in the usage of soy, and it is everywhere from tofu to protein bars and ice creams, etc. Soy stops our body from absorbing minerals. It can also interfere with your thyroid leaving you susceptible to brain fog and weight gain.

Yes, Asian cultures have been using soy for so manycentures, but it is consumed very differently over there as compared to western countries. In Asia, soy is used in small amounts in miso, tempeh and soy sauce but not to the commercial extent of the west.

If you don't have any sensitivity to soy, you can add organic soy to your diet after the 28 days of elimination program.

## Corn

So what's the story with corn? Well, corn has become such a huge part of our diet through corn syrup, dextrose, and the deadliest high-fructose corn syrup. And even if you escape these poisons, corn-fed chicken and beef are all over the place.

Corn raises your blood sugar level just like pure sugar, and guess what happens when you eat eggs or chicken of hens that have been fed corn? Yes, it raises your blood sugar levels.

A lot of people think that by avoiding sugar directly they are doing fine, but you have to be wary of other forms of sugar as well.

And the worse kind of corn is GMO (genetically modified) which is 90% of the corn that is grown in America.

Corn can cause all kind of reactions from itchy skin to depression.

So for the elimination phase, you will be avoiding corn.

## Legumes

Legumes include chickpeas, beans, lentils, peanuts, etc. They are full of lectins which is highly inflammatory, and thus it can cause the same issues as corn and soy which are also full of lectins.

I know people love their peanut butter, but there is a reason that peanut is one of the most notorious allergic food in the world. Commercial peanut butter is full of sugar and sodium to make it taste better. Peanuts also are full of omega-3s (inflammatory fat).

Instead of peanut butter, go for an alternative like almond butter or sunflower butter.

## Nightshade

Nightshade is the name of vines, herbs, and trees that include belladonna and tobacco, etc. Tomatoes, eggplant, bell pepper, hot pepper are also part of this group. Nightshades cause a lot of issues for people with autoimmune disease and arthritis.

For the elimination phase, removing nightshade isn't really required, but I'd recommend that if you already know that you have an autoimmune disease, then you should get rid of them entirely during the 28-day plan.

**Let's go!**

Ok, I hope now you understand that why gluten, eggs, dairy, soy, legumes, corn, sugar, and nightshades are inflammatory. But don't worry I'm going to give you a massive list of food that you can enjoy during the 28-days elimination program so that you can restore balance to your gut.

**The Shopping List**

Vegetables:

- Leafy greens
- Whole vegetables
- Sweet potatoes, beets, pumpkin, butternut
- Sea vegetables
- Peas
- Onion and garlic (small amounts)

Fruit:

- Fresh or frozen berries
- Organic green apples
- Organic oranges
- Organic lemons

Dairy:

- Organic grass-fed ghee
- Hemp and nut milks
- Coconut milk

Grains:

- Quinoa
- Millet
- Buckwheat
- Brown rice
- Rice bran
- Gluten-free oats

Meat and fish:

- Lean, grass-fed beef
- Lamb
- Duck
- Free-range chicken
- Wild caught fish (salmon, sardines)

Nuts and seeds:

- Almonds
- Walnuts
- Hemp
- Pistachio
- Brazil nuts
- Nut butter

Vegetable protein:

- Bee pollen
- Spirulina

Fat and oils:

- Extra-virgin olive oil
- Coconut oil
- Sesame
- Flex
- Almond
- Avocado
- Organic ghee

Drinks:

- Filtered, reverse-osmosis, alkaline water
- Green, white, jasmine, oolong, and herbal teas
- Coconut water
- Juiced green veggies

Sweeteners:

- Limited amounts of stevia, xylitol, erythritol
- Trace amounts of honey, maple syrup

## Condiments:

- All herbs/spices
- Raw, dairy free, sugar-free chocolate
- Ground mustard
- Organic apple cider vinegar
- Fennel seeds

# PART II

# THE GUT C.A.R.E. PROGRAM: TWENTY-EIGHT DAYS TO A NEW YOU

# 1. ELIMINATE SYMPTOMS AND MAINTAIN YOUR HEALTH WITH THE GUT C.A.R.E. PROGRAM

So now that we know what is wrong with your gut let's start repairing it so that you can feel less tired, bloated and exhausted. I can assure you that if you give this program a chance, it will relieve the majority of if not all of your autoimmune problems. All you need is to commit to change your life, and the program will take care of the rest.

So as a reminder here's what C.A.R.E. stands for:

Cleanse: Get rid of toxins from your food.

Activate: Add essential nutrients.

Restore: Reintroduce good bacteria
Enhance: Heal your intestinal lining.

We'll go over each component to give you an overview. It's a gut reboot system that will restore the balance of your gut flora.

So why 28-days? Fair question, the reason is that it takes about two weeks for your body to heal itself from the inflammatory food that you've been eating. Your healing might begin faster than 2 weeks but some might take longer, but if you go 28 days, I can assure you that you will get the maximum benefit from this diet.

This program is designed to help you lose bloat, lose weight and feel younger and energized. The first week might be the hardest, as your body will try to detoxify you of all your toxins. The last 2 weeks are when the healing takes place as your body regenerates the tight connections between your cells to get rid of leakiness.

I know that people are extremely busy nowadays, but you must find time for yourself. You have to make time to get healthy or make time to get sick in the future. The choice is yours!

So let's begin with the C.A.R.E. program.

# Cleanse

So in the first step, get rid of all the unhealthy food and substances from your diet as we discussed in the previous chapter. Also, replace your negative thoughts with positive ones. I'd recommend that you also look into meditation as a way of relaxing.

Alcohol, coffee, and any drugs are also to be avoided during this program. Even some healthy foods have been omitted during this phase but don't worry we can reintroduce them at a later stage once you've finished the program.

So what are the main principles behind happy gut diet? In a nutshell, a happy gut diet focuses on foods that are very easy to digest, low in sugar and don't put a burden on your gut. Allowed foods are non-processed, organic, and non-GMO.

The best part about this diet is that you don't have to count calories. When you aren't putting inflammatory foods in your body, your body tends to function properly and starts regulating your weight without any caloric restrictions.

Another thing that a lot of people might overlook is that I want you to drink clean water during this process. Our tap water is highly contaminated with chemicals, antibiotics and sex hormones.

Better water choices are:

- Carbon filters such as Brita, Aquasana, etc
- Distilled water
- Reverse osmosis system

Also make sure that you are using PFOA-free, PTFE-free kitchen utensils as they have been shown to increase diabetes and obesity rates in the world. For storing your food, avoid plastic containers as much as you can, use glass instead.

For washing dishes, use a plant-based detergent.

Try to minimize your usage of the microwave because it decreases the nutritional value of your food and it also leaks microwaves which can make people feel fatigued.

While you're getting rid of different toxins from your diet, start cleansing your mind of negative thoughts as well. I want you to start doing positive affirmations and tell our inner voice that you will become healthier and you will feel fantastic.

The first step to cleanse your mind would be to start a gratitude journal. Start by writing things that you're grateful for, I'd suggest doing that first thing in the morning, but you can do it whenever you get a chance. Start writing into your gratitude journal on a daily basis and you'll begin to feel different in a matter of a few weeks.

You can also make a vision board to motivate yourself. A vision board is merely a collection of quotes, pictures that inspire you and the things that you want to achieve.

So here's the summary of how to implement the cleanse:

1. Eliminate all allergic food listed in chapter 2, along with alcohol and coffee.
2. Take the gut C.A.R.E. supplement (summarized at the end of the chapter) 3 times daily before meals
3. Prepare gut C.A.R.E. to cleanse shake (sample recipes at the end)
4. Drink clean water
5. Greener kitchen
6. Cleanse your mind

**ACTIVATE**

In this step, you will reactivate the balance in your gut by adding supplements that will replenish enzymes, stomach acids, and fiber. Main enzymes that might require replacement are:

Amylases – Converts carbs into glucose
Proteases – Converts protein to amino acid
Lipases – Breaks down fat

Usually, these are released by the liver, gallbladder, and pancreas, but when your gut is inflamed, these organs don't function properly.

So by adding digestive enzyme supplements, you'll begin breaking down nutrients properly, and then there is no more leakage in your gut.

So here's a summary of how to implement activate:
1. Use gut C.A.R.E. activate digestive enzyme support 3 times daily, 15 mins before each meal.
2. If you've low stomach acid, add a betaine HCl supplement.
3. Have a happy gut breakfast smoothie
4. See a functional medicine practitioner for additional advice.
5. Use gut C.A.R.E. relax supplement for better bowel movements.

**Restore**

In the third step, we will restore the balance in our gut by providing it with proper probiotics to help flourish good flora. Every single time that you have taken antibiotics in your life, it has messed up with your gut flora. A healthy gut flora doesn't only help with your digestion but also with your overall health and mood.

Healthy probiotics help you maintain proper intestinal function. And they also prevent the colonization of bad gut bacteria that may cause ailments.

Ancient cultures throughout the world have taken probiotics. I'd also like to mention that you can take dairy based probiotics even if you're lactose intolerant because of the fermentation.

Some examples are:

- Yogurts, Kefir
- Fermented food
- Beverages such as kombucha, lassi, etc

You should also be taking a probiotic supplement, more on this later. A combination of fermented foods, drinks and supplements might be required if your gut is sick.

Probiotics are non-digestible fibers and found in plenty of foods. And it'd be a good idea to incorporate some of these in your diet.

Here are some examples:

- Raw chicory root
- Raw Jerusalem artichoke
- Raw dandelion greens
- Raw garlic
- Raw onions
- Asparagus
- Banana

Remember to really chew your probiotic food as it'll greatly help with digestion.

Soluble fibers are also a great addition to any diet as they help with slowing down the rate of insulin release in your body. It also lowers your bad cholesterol (LDL).

Here are some examples:

- Apples
- Beans
- Blueberries
- Carrots
- Celery
- Cucumber
- Lentils
- Nuts
- Oat bran
- Oranges
- Psyllium

When you're increasing your fiber intake, make sure that you are increasing your water intake as well because fiber absorbs water.

You should also include some insoluble fibers in your diet, they significantly prevent constipation and help regulate your bowel movements.

Here are some great options:

- Broccoli
- Brown rice
- Cabbage
- Carrots
- Cucumbers
- Dark, leafy greens
- Fruits
- Nuts
- Whole grains

You should be taking in at least 25 grams of fiber in your daily diet. For men, that number is more like 35 grams.

So here are the steps to implement restore in your daily life.

1. Take gut C.A.R.E. restore supplement once daily
2. Take dairy-free probiotics with at least 15 billion CFU's
3. Introduce probiotic food in your life
4. Add cultured foods like kefir
5. Take 9 daily servings of vegetables and fruit

6. Eat the full-color rainbow of fruits and vegetables

## Enhance

Now we will focus on enhancing the function of our gut and our immune system. This step is all about repairing the damage that has already occurred to our gut lining.

We had already started that process by using cleanse when we stopped consuming toxic food. Then we activated proper gut function by introducing good enzymes and nutrients. In restore, we introduced probiotics which will further heal our gut. Now finally in enhance we will finish the process by restoring the tight connection between cells to keep toxic materials from leaking in our body.

Your gut lining may tend to quickly get damaged, but it also has a restoring capability. Given the right environment, your body tends to heal itself.

Following are the ingredients that will help with that:

# L-Glutamine

It is one of the most commonly found amino acids in the body. If we are deficient in L-Glutamine, then our small intestine starts to degenerate. It has been shown in studies to repair the small intestine.

Start with 1 gram of L-Glutamine and dissolve it in water and drink on an empty stomach before eating any meal of the day. You can increase the dose to a maximum of 9 grams if needed.

# DGL (Deglycyrrhizinated Licorice)

It has been shown to have antiulcer, anti-inflammatory and antidiabetic properties and it also protects your stomach lining.

You can add 500 milligrams of DGL to your L-glutamine powder along with aloe vera to make a potent concoction.

It also comes in tablet form as well.

## Aloe Vera

Aloe vera has been used as a healing agent since ancient times. It offers anti-inflammatory and cellular protective properties that help the gut.

Here is how to take it:

Add 100 milligrams to the L-Glutamine and DGL powder or take the gut C.A.R.E. enhance supplement which contains all three of them.

## Essential fatty acids

Omega-3 fatty acids promote anti-inflammation in the bodies. It can even reverse mucosal injury. It helps your neurons make better connections in your brain and fights the inflammation caused by the typical western diet.

Here is how to take it:

1. Take 2-4 1000 milligram softgels daily

2. Add cold water, wild caught fish to your diet

It is also important to keep your omega-3 supplements refrigerated.

## Zinc Carnosine

An average American is very deficient in zinc and this deficiency can cause damage to your stomach lining and can also promote inflammatory diseases.

Take 30 to 50 mg of zinc daily with food.

So finally, here are the steps to implement enhance in your life.

1. Take gut C.A.R.E. enhance or L-glutamine, DGL, aloe vera supplements.
2. Drink a shot of aloe vera every morning
3. Take omega-3s
4. Take a zinc supplement

So that is the complete gut C.A.R.E. program.

You will be implementing it for the next 28 days, and you can also use it in future whenever you feel like you need detox or a cleanse. It will help you lose those dreaded holiday pounds and shed that fat.

Here is a sample day on your happy gut routine:

## Morning

- Wake up with gratitude and set up your goals for the day. Write down what you are grateful for.
- Spend 5-10 minutes on a yoga pose
- Meditate for 5 minutes
- Add half a lemon to a warm glass of water and drink it

## Breakfast

- Drink a morning shake with protein powder and supplements. (Sample recipes at the end)(Use only recommended protein powder)(You can add variety but stick to the recommended foods)

## Lunch

- A meal with a combination of foods from chapter 2, 3, 4.

## Snack

- Raw or steamed vegetables
- Nuts
- 1 teaspoon of coconut oil
- Hummus with raw carrots

## Dinner

- A meal, incorporating the principles of the happy gut diet.

## Supplement routine

## Before morning smoothie

- 1 complete digestive enzyme support
- 1 probiotic

## With morning smoothie

- 1-2 scoops of protein powder
- 1 gut-repair powder
- 2 high potency omega-3 softgels
- 1 plant-based multivitamin
- 1 herbal microbial balancer

## Before lunch

- 1 digestive enzyme support

## With lunch

- 1 herbal microbial balancer

## Before dinner

- 1 digestive enzyme support
- 1 gut repair powder
- 1 probiotic

## With dinner

- 2 omega-3 sfotgels
- 1 herbal microbial balancer

## Before bed
- 1 magnesium citrate
- 1 Triphala
- 30 milliliters aloe vera juice
- Or 1 gut C.A.R.E. relax supplement which contains all three.

Please consider leaving a review if you're enjoying this title.
Thanks.

## 2. TIPS FOR SUCCESS: CREATING A HAPPY GUT

So now that you fully understand the program, it's time to start implementing it for the next 28 days. The first thing you need to do is to eliminate all the regular food that you were eating before and replace it with foods from the diet plan. Keep in mind that the first few days are going to be hardest as your body is going to detoxify itself from all the toxins that you have been putting in your body for years.

The most important thing in any meal plan is to eat foods that you enjoy. I think I've provided you with enough options that you can pick foods of your liking for these 28 days.

Remember, consistency is everything!

Also, don't panic if you notice any detox symptoms because of abstaining from foods that you have always eaten. You will get cravings even headaches. I want you to stick with the plan as all these symptoms will eventually go away. You will start to feel sharper and less foggy in your head, and your energy levels will go up as well.

With the carefully created gut C.A.R.E. program you will be able to detoxify your body in a significant way. You will be getting rid of toxins, extra water weight and will feel way less bloated.

How you eat is also very important. When you are eating, slow down. Try to chew down your food and enjoy each bite.

When you are filling your plate, fill one-quarter with protein and omega-3 foods and fill the rest with greens and veggies.

Another great rule is never to let the food touch the edges of your plate, that will ensure that you aren't overeating. You can also go for smaller plates if you are trying to lose weight.

You should chew your food to the point that it

becomes a soft pulp in your mouth, it will significantly help with the digestion.

Also, try not to drink too much water during your meals as it may dilute your stomach acid.

When you are swallowing your food, don't gulp it down because then you also swallow air with your food which may make you uncomfortable later.

It's also tough to overeat when you're chewing down and swallowing your food slowly.

Stop once you feel that you are about 75% full and wait a few minutes to see if you want to eat more or you are full.

Ok, now let's talk about your lifestyle. In the modern world, we are so overstressed all the time and are always in a rush. For a happy gut, it is vital to fixing your lifestyle as well.

The first thing that you need to pay attention to is proper sleep. Not getting enough sleep or irregular sleep disturbs your circadian rhythm which in turn messes up your metabolism and your gut function. It's extremely important to get good sleep at regular hours every day.

Another major factor that affects in the modern world is stress. Stress causes inflammation regardless of your diet. In chapter 8, I'm going to offer some de-stressors that will help you out.

# PART III

# REINTRODUCTION PHASE AND FURTHER TESTING

# 1. REINTRODUCTION AND YOUR GUT C.A.R.E. PLAN FOR LIFE

After you are done with the 28 days gut C.A.R.E. plan, it is time to re-introduce some foods that you weren't able to eat during those days. In this phase, you will have to pay close attention to how certain foods make you feel, so I'd recommend you to add food slowly.

Reintroduce food in this order:

1. Organic, free-range eggs
2. Organic, rBGH-free dairy
3. Non-GMO corn
4. Non-GMO Soy
5. Legumes
6. Wheat/gluten

Add one food every four days and eat the food more than once during the day to see how you react to it. If you notice that you are feeling some adverse symptoms such as foggy head, sleepy, then you will have to avoid that food.

You will have to get really in tune with your body and trust me it's worth it. So if after the four days you don't notice any symptoms then you can add the next food and so on.

You must have noticed that I didn't talk about re-introducing sugar. Sugar is the root of all evil as far as our health is concerned. Honey or maple syrup can be introduced again but in insufficient quantities. Basically avoid sugar as much as you can.

If you are reacting negatively to all these foods, I'd suggest you get back on the happy gut diet and the gut C.A.R.E. supplements to further heal your gut. In chapter 6, I'll go over what tests you should go under to see what is going on with your gut.

So after you have gone through this whole process, you must clearly understand which foods are causing you adverse symptoms and which foods make you feel fantastic. Also, it is always best to work with your family doctor and nutritionist.

Always keep listening and paying attention to your gut as it will keep evolving. You can switch thing around but still keep the principles of happy gut diet in your mind.

# 2. FURTHER TESTING FOR GUT-RELATED AILMENTS

You might be suffering from a lot of symptoms, and it might be hard to notice which foods are causing those issues. You might be on several medications which could be masking the symptoms while not treating the actual causes.

This chapter is going to introduce you to several diagnostic tests, but it is not important to go through these tests to start the happy gut diet. These tests should be used to refine any problems with your gut further. If your symptoms aren't entirely relieved after the 28 days plan, then this chapter will also help you to diagnose any more issues.

Following are some tests that everyone should get familiarized with:

- CBC (complete blood count) – This is a test for white and red blood cell count.
- Iron profile – This test is used to measure

iron deficiency.
- Fasting glucose – This is used to measure if you have diabetes.
- CMP (complete metabolic profile) – This measures the proper functioning of liver, gallbladder, and kidneys.
- Amylase/Lipase – This shows the level of inflammation in the pancreas.
- Insulin level – This test measures the level of insulin produced by our body.
- Thyroid function tests – A slow thyroid results in hair loss, constant fatigue, and slow metabolism. This test measures the T3 and T4 levels in our bodies.
- Thyroid antibodies – It is essential to test for thyroid antibodies as it can have a significant impact on your health.
- Vitamin D – It is a hormone and is very important in the proper functioning of our immune system.
- Trace minerals – These are zinc, selenium, and magnesium. You test for these by observing your red blood cell level.

The approach in a happy gut diet program can help even a very sick person. The tests that I'm discussing in this chapter will help you pinpoint the imbalances.

Following are tests that I'd recommend for ailments:

- Celiac workshop
- Stool analysis
- Intestinal permeability assessment
- Delayed food sensitivity test
- Colonoscopy
- Thyroid function tests
- Small intestine bacterial overgrowth breath test

Let's look at different causes of gut dysfunctionality.

You react badly to food in two significant ways. Immediate reaction and delayed reaction.

Food intolerance is just like lactose intolerance which means that it results due to an enzyme deficiency.

Signs are:
- Gas
- Bloating
- Flatulence etc.

Food allergies result in an immediate reaction just like a bee sting and are different from a food sensitivity.

Signs are:
- Skin rash
- Hives
- Shortness of breath

Another type of food reaction is known as sensitivity. It is a delayed reaction and thus is very hard to diagnose.

Signs are:

- Delayed symptoms (few hours to 36 hours)
- Hives
- Fatigue
- Mental fog
- Migraines

Because the symptoms show up very late, it is vital to keep track of your signs in a notebook or a computer.

One more food intolerance that we must talk about is gluten intolerance. It is one of the most significant factors in inflammation of the gut.

Signs are:

- Bloating
- Abdominal pain
- Diarrhea
- Weight gain

Also, celiac disease has been linked to:

- Diabetes
- Migraines
- Arthritis

Many people also suffer from lactose , and it is very easy to diagnose because as soon as someone who is lactose intolerant removes dairy from his diet, he immediately starts feeling better. Also, a diagnostic breath test is very beneficial in testing if you're lactose intolerant.

Eliminating dairy during your happy gut program will help you notice if you have any sensitivities towards dairy.

Gut imbalances will also cause all sorts of symptoms. They could be happening due to toxic food or the environment or a deficiency in one of the digestive juices or enzymes.

If you have a stomach acid imbalance, you will immediately feel a hear burn or bloating in your upper abdomen also commonly known as acid reflux as soon as you have a meal. The best remedy for acid reflux is a proper diet.

Another issue that quite a few people face is an intolerance to FODMAPs which are present in many foods and make them hard to digest because they attract water.

Such foods include:

- Lactose
- Fructose
- Sugar alcohols

Symptoms include:

- Gas
- Burping
- Abdominal pain

A diet low in FODMAPs has been shown to help people with weak digestion really and even helps with inflammation greatly.

A very commonly found gastrointestinal disorder is dysbiosis. It is an imbalance in your gut where unwanted bacteria have taken over the whole system. The problem with dysbiosis is that it develops over time and so is very hard to diagnose.

Antibiotics are the main reason that so many people are suffering from dysbiosis. Other reasons could be chronic constipation, stress, chronic indigestion.

Signs of dysbiosis are:

- Diarrhea
- Constipation
- Gas
- Bloating
- Rashes
- Hives
- Nerve pain or numbness in your hands and feet

Another type of dysbiosis is called SIBO which stands for small intestine bacterial overgrowth. It is caused due to the overgrowth of unwanted bacteria in the small intestine.

The most prominent sign of SIBO is when you can't consume any carbohydrates without facing signs like:

- Gas
- Bloating
- Swollen belly

Yeast overgrowth and candidiasis are other forms of dysbiosis. A diet full of carbohydrates and simple sugars is usually the reason for these.

Symptoms are:

- Chronic fatigue
- Mental fog
- Insomnia or oversleeping
- Muscle and joint pain
- Bloating

If you are diagnosed with candidiasis or yeast overgrowth, you have to extra careful about not consuming sugar. You will be very sensitive to even a very trace amount of sugar.

Millions of Americans suffer from acid reflux if you're one of those unfortunate people. The first thing that you should pay attention to before you turn to any medication is your lifestyle and diet. You should also make sure that you are not suffering from Helicobacter pylori with is a very common infection which may cause acid reflux.

Signs are:

- Nausea
- Vomiting
- Abdominal pain

It is transmitted readily through kissing or even sharing a glass.

Low stomach acid is often falsely taken as acid reflux because when you have weak stomach acid, you don't digest the food properly and it just sits in your stomach which will result in your food being pushed upwards.

Signs are:

- Bloating
- Multiple food allergies
- Undigested food in your stool

The most prominent sign of low stomach acid is a bloated stomach right after eating a protein-rich meal. Try taking a betaine hydrochloride supplement during a protein-rich meal and see how you feel afterward.

Ok, the next thing we are going to talk about is enzymes deficiency. Enzymes help break the food in our stomach, and the signs of the deficiency include:

- Stress
- Malnutrition
- Imbalanced stomach pH
- Inflammation
- Fullness lasting 2-4 hours after a meal
- Clay-colored fatty stools

The chronic effects of having an enzymes deficiency are way beyond these symptoms. If you are unable to digest your food properly, you will have several nutrient deficiencies, dysbiosis and protein deficiency.

The pancreas creates its enzyme which is very important for the breakdown of proteins and fat. A deficiency in that particular enzyme will lead to:

- Bloating
- Indigestion
- Abdominal or back pain
- Light colored stools

One of the best ways to self-diagnose is to take a pancreatic enzyme supplement during a fatty meal, and if you were deficient you would not feel your symptoms, and your stool will be solid and brown.

Finally, to accurately diagnose and test for all these issues I'd suggest you see your family doctor along with a functional medicine practitioner.

# PART IV

# A HAPPY GUT, HAPPY LIFE

# 1. THE EMOTIONAL GUT: THE MIND-GUT CONNECTION

The health of your gut doesn't just affect your skin, digestion or your immune system. It has a profound effect on your mind as well. Once you clear up your gut problems, you will relieve yourself from mental issues such as mental fog, inability to concentrate and even depression in a lot of cases.

The gut is called a second brain for a reason. By following the gut C.A.R.E., you will be well on your way to optimal gut health.

You'd be surprised to know that the gut has its nervous system just like the brain. It helps the contraction of muscle cells that line your intestine and opens up the circulation to the gut after you eat.

The connection between mind and the gut is a two-way street. When you have a nervous mind, you tend to get a nervous stomach, but it works the other way as well. When you have a leaky gut with poor digestion, it greatly affects how you feel inside your brain. Gut issues can cause behavioral and psychological changes. In my practice whenever I see a patient with psychiatric and behavioral disorders, the first thing I pay attention to is their gut health.

I truly believe that a vast majority of your mental or physical ailments will resolve through proper gut health.

Here are some the factors how your gut is affecting your mind:

- Dysbiosis: It slows down your thinking ability and affects your memory.
- Leaky gut symptoms.
- Gut response to immune issues such as gluten or lactose.
- Gut inflammation which can cause stress.
- More burden on the liver to detoxify additional toxins.

So the reality is that your mental health is more

connected to your gut health than you thought. So the best way to live a healthy life is to make dietary choices that will not help your gut but your mental health as well.

The gut isn't just connected to our health, but it is also at the forefront of our intuition. You must have heard people talk about their gut feeling. You often get butterflies in your stomach before a big event, it's a very visceral response and is very real. Your second brain a.k.a. your gut tries to communicate with you before your mind gets a hold of your thoughts.

Children are especially experts at this, but as we become adults, we lose our connection with our gut. We should relearn to trust our gut instincts about people and situations as they are more often right than wrong.

Here are the best ways to listen to your gut:

- Listen deeply
- Meditate
- Breathe deeply

- Ground yourself in tough situations
- Practice gratitude

One of the best indicators of having a happy mood is having high serotonin in our bodies. Did you know that your gut has more serotonin receptors than your brain? Actually, 95% of the serotonin in our bodies is produced by our gut. It should then come as no surprise that a happy gut is central to feeling great.

Maybe we should start looking at depression which is caused by the lack of serotonin produced by the body among other factors as a gut related issue rather than a mental one.

A balanced gut bacteria promotes a happy mood, and if that bacteria is out of balance, it will create all sorts of emotional and behavioral problems. Add in your immune system response, and you end up tons of mental and physical issues.

Psychotherapy can significantly help with mental problems, but you must also be working towards reducing inflammation in your body.

Children are especially in danger of having mental problems due to imbalances in guts. It is because they don't have a properly evolved blood-brain barrier yet. Usually, they are given antibiotics which wreak further havoc on their delicate systems. When due to the side effects, they start having trouble at school with concentration they are further labeled as having ADD or autism spectrum disorders and are put on further pills.

Studies have shown that children with autism symptoms have toxins in their guts. There is no one solution for all, but a great place to start diagnosing your kid's health would be to start him on gut C.A.R.E. program.

As we learned before, that the antibiotic overuse leads to candida and yeast overgrowth in our gut. Yeast grows the best on simple carbohydrates which in turn causes issues such as chronic brain fog and fatigue, mood swings and depression. It also creates a leaky gut which allows all the toxins to enter our body freely. The best way to combat yeast overgrowth is to eat a low-sugar, low-carb diet while eating probiotics.

When you have a leaky gut, all the toxins and inflammation quickly spread throughout the whole body. And it also reaches the barrier between the brain's circulation and your body known as the blood-brain barrier which is supposed to keep harmful substances away from your brain and spinal cord.

Once it is damaged though, it will allow these dangerous substances to pass through and cause conditions such as:

- Depression
- Autism
- ADD
- Anxiety
- Chronic pain

If you have a leaky gut, chances are you have a leaky brain. Again the first step towards recovery would be to start on the gut C.A.R.E. program.

Another factor that greatly impacts the health of your gut is stress. Stress causes fight or flight response which is accompanied by increased heart rate, hypersensitive skin and is regulated through cortisol and epinephrine. It can cause gut issues, numbness in your hand and feet, fatigue, high blood pressure among other problems.

One way to counter this is to use a de-stressing exercise such as meditation. Meditation is one of the best practices to adopt in the modern world because we are all run down by too many responsibilities. We usually don't have control over our external circumstances but we can control how we react to those situations and meditation helps with that.

It will also help to relax your gut and improve your digestion by reducing your stress levels.

Start with any mindful meditation practice,

even a few minutes a day would help, and over the time you can increase it.

Meditation is a big part of the gut C.A.R.E. program, and you should continue this practice even after the program. I'll go over a few meditation techniques in the next chapter.

Alternative treatments can also aid your gut health, such as:

- Massage therapy
- Neuromuscular release
- Rolfing
- Acupuncture
- Chiropractic care
- Homeopathy

So you see how your gut is closely related to your mental health. By rebalancing your gut health through gut C.A.R.E., you will also be able to restore your mental functions.

## 2. THE PHYSICAL GUT: THE BODY-GUT CONNECTION

We have lost our ability to be in tune with our bodies in the modern world. We used to move so much more and eat less back when we used to live with other animals in the wilderness. The body-gut connection is about rekindling that relationship again. Movement is key to excellent gut health along with a proper diet.

You can greatly reduce your stress hormones by taking a simple walk in nature. For many exercising has taken the form to go to a gym in a concrete building and running on the treadmill for 30 minutes. Although it is better than doing nothing but the movement is way more than merely going to the gym. You can move your body through so many different ways of taking a dance class to surfing, hiking or playing sports.

Exercise is great to boost your metabolism, building muscles and enhancing your mood.

New research is showing that working out might even benefit your gut microbiome.

Exercise and moving are so deeply ingrained in us that you can say that it is part of our mammalian nature.

One of the best things that you can do to benefit greatly from exercising is by doing yoga. Yoga quiets your mind and allows you to connect with your deep senses. It can help release trigger points in your body which might be causing stress in other areas. It enables you to connect with your body in ways that you might have never experienced before.

When you do yoga, you turn on your PNS (parasympathetic nervous system – calm self) and turn down the SNS (sympathetic nervous system – stress system). It allows your stomach, liver, gallbladder to secrete digestive juices and hormones which promote digestion.

Whenever you're stressed out, you can activate your PNS through breathing, meditation, and yoga. You will notice that when you skip your workouts, you make bad food choices and the opposite is true as well. We want to create the mind-body-gut connection where all three are working in harmony with each other.

The best way to start a yoga practice is by joining a yoga studio or working with a yoga instructor privately. They will help you figure out if you're holding your poses correctly and also how to avoid injury. Once you have successfully learned a few poses, you can start incorporating them into your morning routine before you do your meditation.

You will need the following supplies to start yoga:

- Yoga mat
- Yoga blocks
- Yoga blanket
- Yoga strap

Also learning how to breathe deeply is a great tool to calm your nerves and de-stress. I'd suggest you to start doing a few breathing exercises as well.

You might think that you don't have time for all these practices. I have a saying that you either make time for exercise or make time for getting sick. It's not essential to workout for 2 hours a day, even a 10 minutes' quick workout will be plenty. The most important thing is to keep the practice going on a consistent basis.

My message is simple, go out there and move just like we are supposed to.

# Conclusion

In conclusion, I'd like to say that the gut C.A.R.E. program might seem tedious in the beginning, but it has been revolutionary for so many of my patients. I can say with absolute certainty that it's worth it, your health is worth it, you're worth it. Once you start seeing the benefits with your new found knowledge, you will never want to go back to the same way of eating like before.

You can visit [https://www.happygutlife.com/](https://www.happygutlife.com/) to learn about happy gut friendly recipes and to find great supplements.

Good luck!

Please consider leaving a review if you enjoyed this title.
Thanks.

Made in the USA
Middletown, DE
09 December 2018